INTRODUCTION

Investing money is a way for individuals to save toward their goals, whether it be retirement, a child's college education, or some other financial goal.

Beginning investors need to take time to determine their goals and learn some basic concepts of investing before jumping right into making an investment. Successful investing takes much research, time, and patience.

As beginning investors start to have some success in making money through investments, they will develop a degree of skill. However, there is still a degree of risk involved even the most seasoned and skilled investors. Finding the answers to some basic investing questions will help make the efforts of beginning investors more successful.

One common misconception by beginning investors is that they must have a large sum of money to make an investment. The truth is, many investments can be made for as little as hundreds or perhaps a few thousand dollars. One way to begin investing small is through dividend reinvestment plans or direct stock purchase options.

Investors may be able to invest in a company's stock options by paying a minimal start-up fee, often as little as $25 or $50 and making an initial investment. Once the money begins adding up, it can then be transferred to a brokerage account, where the investor will be able to begin investing larger sums of money.

Once investors determine that they have enough money to make an investment, the difficult part is often deciding where to invest their money. There are many different options for investors; some of the most common investment options are mutual funds, bonds, futures, and real estate.

Most professional investment advisors will confirm that diversification is the key to a successful investment portfolio. Investors who spread their investments out through several avenues reduce their risk of losing all of their assets should the investment fail.

While it may be tempting to dive right in and start investing large sums or money, beginning investors should balance the potential profit against the risks they are exposing themselves to in the investment marketplace.

A professional investment advisor can provide beginning investors with the basic information needed to start an investment portfolio. An investment advisor sometimes is also a financial planner and can help with all financial matters.

Some investment advisors are paid a percentage of the value of the assets managed, while others charge an hourly fee or are paid on a commission basis.

This book is a complete guide on beginning investing covering everything from real estate and stocks to bonds.

Happy Reading.

THE POWER OF INVESTING FOR BEGINNERS

Table of Contents

INTRODUCTION 3
CHAPTER 1 5
    WHAT IS AN INVESTMENT? 5
CHAPTER 2 8
    INVESTMENT AND ITS IMPORTANCE 8
CHAPTER 3 10
    TYPES OF INVESTMENTS 10
CHAPTER 4 13
    INVESTING IN BONDS 13
CHAPTER 5 16
    INVESTING IN MUTUAL FUNDS 16
CHAPTER 6 19
    INVESTING IN A COMMODITY ETF 19
CHAPTER 7 22
    INVESTING IN STOCKS 22
CHAPTER 8 24
    INVESTING IN REAL ESTATE 24
CHAPTER 9 27
    INVESTING IN FUTURES OPTIONS 27
CHAPTER 10 30
    STEPS IN MAKING INVESTMENT PLANS 30
CHAPTER 11 32
    CONSIDERING PERSONAL TAXES 32
CHAPTER 12 34
    INVESTING OVER THE LIFE CYCLE 34
CHAPTER 13 37
    CHOOSE THE BEST INVESTMENT OPTION 37
CONCLUSION 42

CHAPTER 1

WHAT IS AN INVESTMENT?

One of the reasons many people fail, even very woefully, in the game of investing is that they play it without understanding the rules that regulate it. It is an obvious truth that you cannot win a game if you violate its rules.

However, you must know the rules before you will be able to avoid violating them. Another reason people fail in investing is that they play the game without understanding what it is all about.

This is why it is important to unmask the meaning of the term, 'investment'. What is an investment? An investment is an income-generating valuable. It is very important that you take note of every word in the definition because they are important in understanding the real meaning of investment.

From the definition above, there are two key features of an investment. Every possession, belonging or property (of yours) must satisfy both conditions before it can qualify to become (or be called) an investment. Otherwise, it will be something other than an investment. The first feature of an investment is that it is a valuable - something that is very useful or important.

Hence, any possession, belonging or property (of yours) that has no value is not, and cannot be, an investment. By the standard of this definition, a worthless, useless or insignificant possession, belonging or property is not an investment. Every investment has value that can be quantified monetarily. In other words, every investment has a monetary worth.

The second feature of an investment is that, in addition to being a valuable, it must be income-generating. This means that it must be able to make money for the owner, or at least, help the owner in the money-making process. Every investment has wealth-creating capacity, obligation, responsibility and function. This is an inalienable feature of an investment.

Any possession, belonging or property that cannot generate income for the owner, or at least help the owner in generating income, is not, and cannot be, an investment, irrespective of how valuable or precious it may be. In addition, any belonging that cannot play any of these financial roles is not an investment, irrespective of how expensive or costly it may be.

There is another feature of an investment that is very closely related to the second feature described above which you should be very mindful of. This will also help you realize if a valuable is an investment or not. An investment that does not generate money in the strict sense, or help in generating income, saves money.

Such an investment saves the owner from some expenses he would have been making in its absence, though it may lack the capacity to attract some money to the pocket of the investor.

By so doing, the investment generates money for the owner, though not in the strict sense. In other words, the investment still performs a wealth-creating function for the owner/investor.

As a rule, every valuable, in addition to being something that is very useful and important, must have the capacity to generate income for the owner, or save money for him, before it can qualify to be called an investment. It is very important to emphasize the second feature of an investment (i.e. an investment as being income-generating).

The reason for this claim is that most people consider only the first feature in their judgments on what constitutes an investment. They understand an investment simply as a valuable, even if the valuable is income-devouring. Such a misconception usually has serious long-term financial consequences. Such people often make costly financial mistakes that cost them fortunes in life.

It is a pity that many people, especially financially ignorant people, consider valuables that consume their incomes, but do not generate any income for them, as investments.

Such people record their income-consuming valuables on the list of their investments. People who do so are financial illiterates. This is why they have no future in their finances.

What financially literate people describe as income-consuming valuables are considered as investments by financial illiterates. This shows a difference in perception, reasoning and mindset between financially literate people and financially illiterate and ignorant people. This is why financially literate people have future in their finances while financial illiterates do not.

From the definition above, the first thing you should consider in investing is, "How valuable is what you want to acquire with your money as an investment?" The higher the value, all things being equal, the better the investment (though the higher the cost of the acquisition will likely be).

The second factor is, "How much can it generate for you?" If it is a valuable but non income-generating, then it is not (and cannot be) an investment, needless to say that it cannot be income-generating if it is not a valuable.

Hence, if you cannot answer both questions in the affirmative, then what you are doing cannot be investing and what you are acquiring cannot be an investment. At best, you may be acquiring a liability.

CHAPTER 2

INVESTMENT AND ITS IMPORTANCE

Investment is important from many points of view. Before doing investment, it is essential to understand its importance.

Need of Investment

The investment can help you in the future if invested wisely and properly. As per human nature, we plan for a few days or think to plan for investment, but do not put the plan into action. Every individual must plan for investment and keep aside some amount of money for the future.

No doubt, the future is uncertain and it is required to invest smartly with some certain plan of actions that can avoid financial crisis at point of time. It can help you to bring a bright and secure future. It not only gives you secure future, but also controls your spending pattern.

Important Factors of Investments

Planning for Financial investment - Planning plays a pivotal role in all fields. For the financial investment, one must have a pertinent plan by taking all rise and fall situations of the market.

You should have a good knowledge of investment before planning for financial investment. Keen observation and focused approach are the basic needs for successful financial investment.

Invest according to your Needs and Capability- The purpose behind the investment should be clear by which you can fulfill your needs from the investment.

In investment, financial ability is also a component that can bring you satisfaction and whatever results you want. You can start investment from a small amount as per your capability. You should care about your income and stability to choose the best plan for you.

Explore the market for available investment options - The investment market is full of opportunities, you can explore the market by applying proper approach.

You can take help from financial planners, managers who have thorough knowledge about investment in the market. Explore the possibility of investment markets and touch the sublime height of success by the sensible investment decisions.

By taking help from an experienced, proficient financial planner and traders can also give you confidence to do well in the field of investment. Now the question strikes the mind that what are the types of investments?

CHAPTER 3
TYPES OF INVESTMENTS

When you decide to join the world of investing, there are a lot of factors that you need to consider and think over. Aside from the where you would like to invest and the amount of valuables you are willing to risk, you also have to consider which type of investments you want to pursue. Yes, there are different types of investments that you can gauge and consider.

There are two types of investments done in the trading market. These two major classification falls under short term investments and long term investments. If you find yourself more confused in choosing which to choose among these two types of investments, simply be aware of the differences and the pros and cons and you will be on the right track.

Basically the major differences between these two types of investments are that short term plans are designed to show a substantial return in a short period of time. Long-term investments meanwhile, are investments designed to last for a few years or so and present a slow, steady progressive increase in its yields.

With the main difference between these two types of investments stated, the disadvantages and advantages of each should also be known and weighed.

The first of the two types of investments is short term investments which has great potentials of growth and increase in value over a very fast period of time ranging only from a few weeks to a few months.

Although it might face the challenges of fluctuations trends in the market, short term investments still allows more personal control since it is likely that you will be the one to keep an eye on your money.

Its weakness meanwhile is it will prove to be riskier due to the shifts in an unpredictable market. Compared to its counterpart, this is more prone to volatile circumstances because of its lifespan. So even if the chance of greater yields is aimed for, there are also greater chances of risks that you lose a lot of money.

Long-term investments on the other hand provide steady and reliable yields for the future retirement years. It gains small and distributed profits over a longer period of time. Thanks to its slow-but-steady pace, it is seen to be a lot stable and it involves lesser risks along the way too.

One disadvantage though of long-term investments is since profit cannot be expected right away; this particular investment will not be an option for you if you are in dire need of money during emergency situations.

Aside from this, it would be expected that you would have lesser control over your money because the maturity date of your investment is not immediate. Also, it would be expected that there are fees to be paid while the investment is making its way to its maturity date.

There are several less-risky options if you are considering investing money for a future event such college for your children or retirement, If you are planning for a long-term investment, then there are many different investments that will show a decent return over time.

Bonds are one of the safest ways to invest. They are like purchasing CDs or Certificates of Deposit. However, bonds are issued by the government, not banks. Your investment could double over a specific period of time depending on the type of bonds in which you choose to invest, though obviously all the usual caveats apply - there are no guarantees.

Mutual funds are when a group of investors put their money together and buy bonds, stock, and other types of investments. If you find a qualified, reputable broker who can handle mutual funds and will invest them for you and decide on a fund manager who will decide how the money is invested, then you will be able to invest in mutual funds.

They are a little riskier than bonds, but not as risky as the stock market. Again, it's a question of whether you feel confident enough to take charge of your own destiny or leave it in the hands of others.

If you are looking for another type of long-term investment, then shares or stocks may be something to consider. When you purchase stock, you are purchasing part ownership of the company in which you are investing. If the company does well, then the stock goes up and you will make more money.

On the other hand, if the company does not do so well, and it loses money in profits, then your stock value drops and you lose money, too. There are some reliable companies that have been around for a long time that you can invest in and your money will remain relatively safe, but it may not grow quickly. Using methods such as moving averages can help you successfully follow upward trends.

Looking at the choices, you may decide to invest in a little of each type listed above. Do considerable research when investing for the long-term gain. When choosing a stock, it is best to start with a business that is well-established. When deciding to invest in mutual funds, be sure that the broker has a good track record for past performance before handing your money over.

If you are not sure you want to take a big investment risk in the stocks or mutual funds, then go with the government guaranteed bonds. It is not as fast and as big of a return, but you will get a return and you won't be in as much danger of losing your investment.

CHAPTER 4

INVESTING IN BONDS

When you buy a bond, you are actually loaning your money to the organization that issued the bond. That is why bonds are often called "debt instruments."

The principal (the "face value" of the bond) is repaid on the maturity date. In the meantime, you are paid a set amount of interest, usually every six months. This interest is called the "coupon" or "coupon rate."

It's called that because bonds used to come with little coupons attached that you would cut off and send in twice a year to receive the interest payment. Nowadays, the coupon rate is nothing more than the annual interest rate.

When deciding which types of bonds to invest in, it's important to know all you can about each. Among the types of bonds you can choose from are:

Treasury Bonds

Treasury bonds, also known as "T-bonds" for short, are issued by the United States government and are considered to be the safest of the three bonds. The only risk is if they are sold prior to maturity (but this holds true for all bonds). Super-safety comes at a cost, though, and in the case of treasury bonds that means lower returns than other bonds.

Interest is paid on treasury bonds twice a year, and can be purchased in maturities ranging up to 30 years. All T-bonds bonds are issued in face values of $1,000 with different purchase minimums with each type of security. It is impossible to redeem a treasury bond before maturity, and interest payments stop as soon as the bonds mature.

Corporate

Corporate bonds are issued by companies in order to raise capital. While they can be very safe investments when issued by strong, established companies, the reverse is true for companies that are not rock solid. Unlike treasury bonds, corporate bonds have what is known as a "call provision", which allows the bond holder to get their principle investment back before maturity.

Most corporate bonds have fixed interest rates, and some, called "zero coupons" are sold at a significant discount in exchange for the bondholder agreeing to wait until maturity to receive interest payments.

Because determining which companies are strong and which aren't can be very tricky, there are companies who evaluate the fiscal integrity of various corporations to determine their bond-worthiness. Moody's Investors Services and Standard and Poor are two examples of such rating companies.

Municipal

Municipal bonds are issued by state, county, or city governments for the purpose of financing government sponsored functions (I.E., building a highway or a school), or for other "non-governmental" purposes, such as raising money for low income housing or student loans.

Municipal bonds, like T-bonds, pay interest twice a year. These investments can be very safe, but do carry risks as well. Moody's and Standard & Poor rate municipal bonds based on their credit ▢uality, so when investing in them, it's a very good idea to use these ratings as a guideline.

Municipal bonds are subject to significant market risk if sold before maturity.

Maintaining a Diversified Portfolio

Many personal financial advisors recommend that investors maintain a diversified investment portfolio consisting of bonds, stocks and cash in varying percentages, depending upon individual circumstances and objectives.

Because bonds typically have a predictable stream of payments and repayment of principal, many people invest in them to preserve and increase their capital or to receive dependable interest income.

Whatever the purpose-saving for your children's college education or a new home, increasing retirement income or any of a number of other financial goals-investing in bonds can help you achieve your objectives.

Assessing Risk

All investments offer a balance between risk and potential return. The risk is the chance that you will lose some or all the money you invest. The return is the money you stand to make on the investment.

The balance between risk and return varies by the type of investment, the entity that issues it, the state of the economy and the cycle of the securities markets. As a general rule, to earn the higher returns, you have to take greater risk. Conversely, the least risky investments also have the lowest returns.

The bond market is no exception to this rule. Bonds in general are considered less risky than stocks for several reasons:

Bonds carry the promise of their issuer to return the face value of the security to the holder at maturity; stocks have no such promise from their issuer.

Most bonds pay investors a fixed rate of interest income that is also backed by a promise from the issuer. Stocks sometimes pay dividends, but their issuer has no obligation to make these payments to shareholders.

Historically the bond market has been less vulnerable to price swings or volatility than the stock market.

The average returns from bond investments have also been historically lower, if more stable, than average stock market returns.

CHAPTER 5

INVESTING IN MUTUAL FUNDS

Even if you don't really understand stocks and bonds and the markets they trade in, you and other beginners can make money investing in mutual funds once you get a handle on the mutual funds universe. Here we take the mystery out of investing for beginners.

Tens of millions of Americans make money investing in mutual funds without knowing what they are doing. Caution: They also lose money unnecessarily and they are not investing as beginners, because they have been doing it for years. Let's look at what you really need to know to make money investing on a more consistent basis while avoiding serious losses.

Mutual funds were created and promoted as the average investor's vehicle for investing money in stocks and bonds. That's just what they are packages of investments managed for investors by professional money managers.

They make investing for beginners simple. You simply open an account, and put your money down with instructions as to how much to invest in which funds.

Example: You send in $10,000 to buy shares of ABC Stock Fund. Soon you will own shares in that fund and will own a very small part of a very large portfolio of stocks. The number of shares you will own will depend on the share price at the time your purchase order is processed.

Whether or not you make money investing in mutual funds without taking much risk depends on which funds you invest money in and how you go about it. There are basically three traditional fund alternatives: stock (diversified), bond, and money market funds.

You should invest in all three types if your goal is to consistently make money investing in mutual funds. You also need to understand asset allocation, so you can tailor your total mutual fund portfolio to fit your risk profile. And remember, investing for beginners need not be difficult.

Diversified stock funds are the riskiest of the three and they are your growth engine for earning higher returns. They invest your money in a broad spectrum of stocks representing a number of different industries. This makes investing for beginners simple compared to picking your own stocks.

You make money investing here primarily through price appreciation (the fund share price going up) and through dividends. The major risk: share prices fluctuate and can fall significantly when the stock market falls. One year you can make 20%, 30% or more; and you can also lose that much. Over the long term, investors have averaged about 10% a year. Notice I said LONG TERM.

Bond funds invest your money in bonds, which are debt securities that pay interest. Their primary objective is not growth, but rather to earn higher interest for investors than they could earn from safe investments like bank CDs.

Traditionally, you make money investing in these mutual funds primarily through the dividends they pay you from the interest they earn. Normally they pay considerably higher dividends than stock funds do, but similar to stock funds their share price fluctuates (usually much less).

You can profit from higher share prices, but you can also lose money here. They are considered to be safer investments than stock funds, but bond funds are not necessarily safe investments.

Money market funds invest your money in high-quality short-term debt instruments (IOUs) and pay current interest rates in the form of dividends. Unlike the other two mutual funds, their share price is pegged at $1 and does not fluctuate by design.

As interest rates go up the dividend increases, and as rates fall so does the dividend. You make money investing in these mutual funds only through the dividends paid. These mutual funds are considered to be safe investments, and can be used as a cash reserve awaiting bigger opportunities.

To make money investing in mutual funds without worrying your head off you should invest in all three to have a balanced investment portfolio. Here's what I mean by balance and why it is so important to investing for beginners. Holding either stock or bond funds involves the risk of losing money.

If you invest in both this will lower your overall risk. Reason: oftentimes losses in one are offset by gains in the other. Money market funds add flexibility and a cushion of risk to your overall portfolio of mutual funds. The more safety you want the more you allocate to money market funds.

An example of investing for beginners follows. You invest $10,000 equally allocated to the three basic fund types. A couple of years later you see that the stock fund is worth quite a bit more than the other two. The good news is that stocks performed very well. The bad news is that a major decline in stock prices could wipe out your profits and more.

To keep things in balance, rebalance once a year so that you are back to equal amounts in each fund. This is very important if you want to make money investing in mutual funds on a consistent basis without unpleasant surprises every few years.

When you invest in Mutual Funds, you are pooling your money with a number of other investors. You then pay someone to professionally manage and choose each individual security for you. There are a variety of different mutual funds you can choose to invest in, which range to fit your investment strategy.

3 Types of Mutual Funds

1.) Open-Ended

2.) Unit Investment Trust

3.) Close-Ended

CHAPTER 6

INVESTING IN A COMMODITY ETF

Exchange Traded Funds, commonly known as ETF's, have taken center stage in the financial arena for the past few years. ETFs give investors a chance to diversify their portfolios with less volatility within a certain market. Commodities ETFs are exactly what the same suggests, a fund populated with components from the commodities sector.

An important note is that commodities EFFs track the actual producers or distributors of commodities rather than commodity ETFs, which track the actual underlying commodity, which firms may hold the actual commodity in storage or via futures contracts. Beyond that, there's a variety of choices.

Precious metals, for example, might have their own ETF, such as Power Shares' Precious Metals ETF (DBP). Or investors might want to get more specific and find an ETF that specializes in gold, silver, or platinum. On the other end of the spectrum, Goldman Sachs' Commodity Index (GSCI) tracks 24 commodities across a variety of sectors.

The strategy on ETFs can vary, too- one ETF in gold might have platforms from a long only strategy to a double short strategy. Agricultural commodities, industrial commodities, and oil are other popular sectors that have commodity ETFs established.

ETFs are a separate asset class from regular stocks and bonds, so including them in your portfolio allows for diversification. In addition, if an investor feels strongly that, say, energy costs will rise this ◻uarter, purchasing oil ETF provides a way to capture a gain on that assumption.

It's important to investigate the tax implications of the ETF you choose, as well as conduct a thorough historical analysis of prices for the specific commodity.

Owning a commodities ETF is a pure lesson in supply and demand; a bet on whether or not an investor thinks a commodity will be more or less profitable in a given amount of time. And commodities ETFs can prove to be volatile, given the sharp flux a commodity can experience in value at a moment's notice.

That being said, investors can capture some great returns, especially in sectors where there's a good chance the commodity will be in demand for the long term.

Some investors also use ETFs to hedge against other investments or inflation; iShares' GLD, a popular gold ETF, is often used to combat the declining value of the dollar in a portfolio.

Commodities ETFs also allow investors to get broad exposure to a commodities market in their portfolio without physically purchasing the commodity (previously, this was how it would have worked).

While not for everyone, for those looking to add a new asset class and element of diversification to their portfolios, Commodities ETFs can be a great fit.

If you investigate the returns of unique assets such as equities, bonds, and real estate, you'll discover that they generally are not highly correlated to commodities. Therefore, by adding commodities to your portfolio, you're diversifying it, and decreasing the probability that the value of all your holdings will decrease simultaneously.

This is great news when stocks are volatile and declining. It also makes perfect sense: commodities represent another "basket" and you diversify by not putting "all your eggs in the same basket." If you're an investment guru, like Warren Buffett, then you don't need to worry about this.

For everyone else, diversification is simply a requirement. Because of the fact that not all assets zig and zag in unison, it guards your portfolio from inevitable market declines.

It used to be challenging to participate in the commodities market. You either needed to be a high net worth individual (due to the large minimum investment amount necessary to establish an account), or you had to be familiar and comfortable with trading commodity futures. This is no longer required.

Any retail investor may now allocate part of his portfolio to commodities by buying a commodity ETF. These exchange traded securities can be traded on a stock exchange and are available through regular brokerage accounts. They trade intra-day, and are bought and sold in the same way that stocks are.

There are now more than one hundred different commodity ETFs, so how do you decide which one to buy? For most investors it makes most sense to buy a broad commodity index fund.

One widely followed commodity index is the S&P Goldman Sachs Commodity Index (GSCI), which tracks 24 different commodity futures contracts. With this single investment, you can track the price of all the most common physical commodities in the world.

When owned as a diversified basket, commodities often have lower volatility than other risky asset classes such as stocks. For example, during the global financial crisis just a few years ago, equities were more than twice as volatile as the S&P GSCI commodity index.

A commodity ETF is an un-leveraged way to benefit from rising prices of commodities. This is very different from trading commodity futures contracts, which involves a lot of leverage: a moderate change in price of the underlying commodity can wipe out your account. This makes commodity ETFs much more suitable for a typical investor.

CHAPTER 7

INVESTING IN STOCKS

The most popular of all investing opportunities, are stocks. Stocks are probably the main thing you think of when you hear of investing. When you buy a stock, you buy partial ownership of a company. Stocks range anywhere from $2, to $12,000, which can appeal to a large variety of people. To be successful when trading stocks, you have to buy low and sell high.

Of course this isn't easy, considering the market is always fluctuating. You need to watch the history of the company, know the PE Ratio, the day range, the 52 week range, etc. Knowing this information can help you predict if the stock will go up or down.

You can make a lot of money investing in stocks, which means you can also lose a lot of money. You want to keep in mind that most investments in stocks are long term investments. It is very risky investing, but if you do the proper research of the history of the company, you can get a very good return.

Stock Investing Tips

1.) Have the Right Expectations

When you are investing in stocks, you want to make sure you aren't expecting to become Warren Buffet over night. It just wont happen. You want to make sure you do the proper amount of research, and make sure you know the history of the market as well as the company you are investing in. When investing in stocks, the return is around 10%-13%.

You don't want to make hasty decisions and buy and sell a lot just because you aren't making the money you expected. Make sure you know how long you are keeping an investment, and then make a commitment. This will help you focus on the principles.

2.) Don't Listen to the Media

Don't get caught up in what everyone is talking about and what is being said around you. It will take your decision from being based on research and history, to just "hear-say".

This will hurt your investments immensely. Most of the hype and other things that are being said are just the daily fluctuation of the market.

3.) Stay Focused

You want to make sure you are putting all your effort and focus into your investments. Once you buy a stock, you own part of a company.

Make sure you treat it the way it is and make sure you do the proper research of all aspects of what you're investing in. Doing your research can change your investment of making a profit of $15,000, to losing $15,000. In the end, it's always worth it to do the extra work.

CHAPTER 8

INVESTING IN REAL ESTATE

Real estate is a popular investment. There are many modifications in the monetary system having puffed-up risk or lesser returns, the investment marketplace go on with the plan imaginative and good-looking investment approaches.

These developments make it important for real estate licenses to have an elementary and up-to-date knowledge of real estate investment.

Of course, this does not mean that licenses should act as investment counselors. For all the time they should refer investors to knowledgeable tax accountants, attorneys, or investment professionals. These are the professionals who can give expert advice on an investor's specific needs.

Consider All the Three Factors Before Investing in Real Estate

The three factors of investing in real estate are area, perception and economics. The key to making the best investment in real estate, and specifically in cooperatives, and townhouses, is to consider all the three factors.

Investing in real estate correspond to a certain commitments on the part of the purchaser. Investment in real estate made solely upon the location of the property will not yield those results. Before making an investment, it is essential to include the three considerations

Consider on the whole area.

Consider awareness of the area.

Consider the financial factors.

Merits of Real Estate Investment:

Real estate values have varied extensively in various areas of the country. Yet many real estate investments have shown above average rates of return, generally greater than the prevailing interest rates charged by mortgage lenders.

In assumption, this means the investor can utilize the influence of rented money to invest a real estate purchase and feel comparatively sure that, if held long enough, the asset will yield more money than it cost to finance the purchase.

Real estate offers investors greater control over their investments than do other options such as stocks etc. Real estate investors also are given assured tax advantages.

Demerits of Real Estate Investment:

Liquidity refers to how quickly an asset may be converted into cash. For instance, an investor in listed stocks has only a call a stockbroker when funds are needed. The stockbroker sells the stock, and the investor receives the cash.

In contract, a real estate investor may have to sell the property at a substantially lower price than desired to ensure a quick sale. Of course, a real estate investor may be able to raise a limited amount of cash by refinancing the property.

Huge amounts are generally necessary to invest in real estate. It is not easy to invest in real estate without professional guidance. Investment decisions must be based on careful studies of all the facts, reinforced by a thorough knowledge of real estate and the manner in which it is affected by the marketplace.

Real estate has need of dynamic administration. A real estate investor can rarely sit idle by and watch his or her money grow. Administration assessments must be made. The investor may want to manage the property personally. On the other hand, it may be preferable to hire a professional property manager. Physical improve

ments accomplished by the investor personally may be required to make the asset profitable. Many good investments fail because of poor management.

Finally, it involves a high degree of risk. The opportunity forever survives that an investor's property will diminish in rate during the time it is held or that it will not make enough income to make it advantageous.

CHAPTER 9

INVESTING IN FUTURES OPTIONS

Those who are dealing with futures options only have a small portion of actual investments which are reflected in their portfolios. This type trading however, gives traders more flexibility as well as versatility.

They are also able to reduce high risk by choosing the most profitable assets that will be included in their portfolios. However, new traders have to do more research in order for them to study commodities that they intend make investments in.

People who are investing in futures options have to learn everything that they can especially on the underlying commodities that are represented only by a specified amount and quantity which is far too less than the actual volume that they are buying or selling at a future date. Traders may choose from a variety of commodities like corn, coffee, cotton, lumber or cattle.

They may also deal with precious metals that include not only gold and silver but also platinum, copper and other materials. Although this is still a part of the trading business, people who invest may earn or may lose in a very short period of time unlike those who are into stocks or bonds investments.

People are actually making agreements on the delivery of the commodities at a predetermined time in the future and on a specific price that has been set. However, these agreements can be very risky especially as prices in the market may fluctuate at any time.

Traders may have the opportunity to buy or to sell the underlying commodities before the specified date in order to protect them from the risk of losing a lot when market trends turn against their investments.

People who are interested in investing may consider futures options especially if they do not have the entire amount to really buy the commodities in its actual volume.

Individuals can trade through a determined fraction of the total cost of the investment. Traders then are given a deadline when they can make the purchase. They may then gain if the price will go up while they are waiting for the set date of the actual purchase.

In case that they price will go down on the other hand, the traders will not be obliged to make the purchase but they will lose in terms of the fees that they have paid for the futures option contract that they have made. Traders have to be careful in making agreements as these are considered as binding contracts that need to be carried out.

The general public perception of trading futures is that it involves a high risk of investment and speculation. Some even regard investing in futures as a form of gambling. While futures do involve a high risk of loss, the irony is that they are also instrumental in reducing risk.

With proper planning, research, analysis and money management, futures trading can be highly profitable. Futures are also used to as a mechanism by companies to manage price risks. This is known as hedging.

Here are 6 reasons why you should consider futures trading as a tool of investment.

1. Leverage

Unlike stocks, trading futures does not require you to enter into a contract with a full value. You will only need to deposit a margin, usually between 5% - 10% of the total contract value. In this manner, you are able to trade larger amounts of commodities than compared to purchasing commodities outright.

2. Higher Returns

Since you are entering a position of a contract with only a margin, when the market movement is towards your favour, the profit can be of ten-fold of the margin. Due to this unique and great leverage, futures trading offers excellent return in comparison to other investment instruments, though the loss may also be substantial.

3. Being a Paper Investment

Futures trading is basically a paper investment. Even though futures trading involves commodities, you will not need to worry about the actual commodities itself, or changing hands of the commodities. This makes it convenient without the concern about the physical commodities and storage.

4. Highly Liquid

Trading futures are considered to be very liquid. There are large amounts of contracts traded in the market daily. You can place an order and they can be bought or sold very quickly. There will always be a significant available number of buyers and sellers for futures contracts.

5. Making Returns When Market Moves Both Ways

When you're trading futures, you will have the option to go long or short. You will be able to profit whether the market is going on an upward trend or a downward trend. You may enter a long position in a bullish market and go short on a bearish market.

6. Timeframe

Apart from the high return of investments, futures trading may also bring you fast returns as opposed to the stock markets where significant returns can be seen after years of investing. This is due to the volatility of the futures market, especially in commodity markets like Crude Palm Oil.

CHAPTER 10

STEPS IN MAKING INVESTMENT PLANS

Steps In Investing

Step 1: Meeting Investment Prerequisites-Before one even thinks of investing, they should make sure they have adequately provided for the necessities, like housing, food, transportation, clothing, etc.

Also, there should be an additional amount of money that could be used as emergency cash, and protection against other various risks. This protection could be through life, health, property, and liability insurance.

Step 2: Establishing Investing Goals-Once the prerequisites are taken care of, an investor will then want to establish their investing goals, which is laying out financial objectives they wish to achieve.

The goals chosen will determine what types of investments they will make. The most common investing goals are accumulating retirement funds, increasing current income, saving for major expenditures, and sheltering income from taxes.

Step 3: Adopting an Investment Plan-Once someone has their general goals, they will need to adopt an investment plan. This will include specifying a target date for achieving a goal and the amount of tolerable risk involved.

Step 4: Evaluating Investment Vehicles-Next up is evaluating investment vehicles by looking at each vehicle's potential return and risk.

Step 5: Selecting Suitable Investments-With all the information gathered so far, a person will use it to select the investment vehicles that will complement their goals the most. One should take into consideration expected return, risk, and tax considerations. Careful selection is important.

Step 6: Constructing a Diversified Portfolio-In order to achieve their investment goals, investors will need to pull together an investment portfolio of suitable investments.

Investors should diversify their portfolio by including a number of different investment vehicles to earn higher returns and/or to be exposed to less risk as opposed to just limiting themselves to one or two investments.

Investing in mutual funds can help achieve diversification and also have the benefit of it being professionally managed.

Step 7: Managing the Portfolio-Once a portfolio is put together, an investor should measure the behavior in relation to expected performance, and make adjustments as needed.

CHAPTER 11

CONSIDERING PERSONAL TAXES

Knowing current tax laws can help an investor reduce the taxes and increase the amount of after-tax dollars available for investing.

Basic Sources of Taxation-There are two main types of taxes to know about which are those levied by the federal government, and those levied by state and local governments. The federal income tax is the main form of personal taxation, while state and local taxes can vary from area to area.

In addition to the income taxes, the state and local governments also receive revenue from sales and property taxes. These income taxes have the greatest impact on security investments, which the returns are in the form of dividends, interest, and increases in value. Property taxes can also have a significant impact on real estate and other forms of property investment.

Types of Income-Income for individuals can be classified into three basic categories:

1. Active Income-This can be made up of wages, salaries, bonuses, tips, pension, and alimony. It is made up of income earned on the job as well as through other forms of noninvestment income.

2. Portfolio Income-This income is from earnings produced from various investments which could be made up of savings accounts, stocks, bonds, mutual funds, options, and futures, and consists of interest, dividends, and capital gains.

3. Passive Income-Income gained through real estate, limited partnerships, and other forms of tax-advantaged investments.

Investments and Taxes-Taking into tax laws is an important part of the investment process. Tax planning involves examining both current and projected earnings, and developing strategies to help defer and minimize the level of taxes. Planning for these taxes will help assist investment activities over time so that an investor can achieve maximum after-tax returns.

Tax-Advantaged Retirement Vehicles-Over the years the federal government has established several types of retirement vehicles. Employer-sponsored plans can include 401(k) plans, savings plans, and profit-sharing plans. These plans are usually voluntary and allow employees to increase the amount of money for retirement and tax advantage of tax-deferral benefits.

Individuals can also setup tax-sheltered retirement programs like Keogh plans and SEP-IRAs for the self-employed. IRAs and Roth IRAs can be setup by almost anyone, subject to certain qualifications. These plans generally allow people to defer taxes on both the contributions and earnings until retirement.

CHAPTER 12

INVESTING OVER THE LIFE CYCLE

As investors age, their investment strategies tend to change as well. They tend to be more aggressive when they're young and transition to more conservative investments as they grow older. Younger investors usually go for growth-oriented investments that focus on capital gains as opposed to current income.

This is because they don't usually have much for investable funds, so capital gains are often viewed as the quickest way to build up capital. These investments are usually through high-risk common stocks, options, and futures.

As the investors become more middle-aged, other things like educational expenses and retirement become more important. As this happens, the typical investor moves towards more higher quality securities which are low-risk growth and income stocks, high-grade bonds, preferred stocks, and mutual funds.

As the investors get closer to retirement, their focus is usually on the preservation of capital and income. Their investment portfolio is now usually very conservative at this point. It would typically consist of low-risk income stocks and mutual funds, high-yield government bonds, quality corporate bonds, CDs, and other short-term investment vehicles.

Investing In Different Economic Conditions

Even though the government has different tools or strategies for moderating economic swings, investors will still endure numerous changes in the economy while investing.

An investment program must allow the investor to recognize and react to changing conditions in the economy. It is important to know where to put your money and when to make your moves.

Knowing where to put your money is the easiest part to deal with. This involves matching the risk and return objectives of an investor's plan with the investment vehicles. For example, if there is an experienced investor that can tolerate more risk, then speculative stocks may be right for them.

A novice investor that wants a decent return on their capital may decide to invest in a growth-oriented mutual fund. Although stocks and growth funds may do well in an expanding economy, they can turn out to be failures at other times. Because of this, it is important to know when to make your moves.

Knowing when to invest is difficult because it deals with market timing. Even most professional money managers, economists, and investors can't consistently predict the market and economic movements. It's easier to understand the current state of the market or economy.

That is, knowing whether the market/economy is expanding or declining is easier to understand than trying to predict upcoming changes.

The market or economy can have three different conditions: (1) recovery or expansion, (2) decline or recession, (3) a change in the general direction of its movement. It's fairly easy to observe when the economy is in a state of expansion or recession. The difficult part is knowing whether the existing state of the economy will continue on the course it's on, or change direction.

How an investor responds to these market conditions will depend on the types of investment vehicles they hold. No matter what the state of the economy is, an investor's willingness to enter the capital market depends on a basic trust in fair and accurate financial reporting.

Stocks and the Business Cycle

Conditions in the economy are highly influential on common stocks and other equity-related securities. Economic conditions is also referred to as the business cycle. The business cycle mirrors the current status of a variety of economic variables which includes GDP, industrial production, personal disposable income, the unemployment rate, and more.

An expanding business cycle will be reflected in a strong economy. When business is thriving and profits are up, stock prices react by increasing in value and returns.

Speculative and growth-oriented stocks tend to do especially well in strong markets. On the flip side, when economic activity is diminishing, the values and returns on common stocks tend to follow the same pattern.

Bonds and Interest Rates

Bonds and other forms of fixed-income securities are highly sensitive to movements in interest rates. The single most important variable that determines bond price behavior and returns is the interest rate.

Bond prices and interest rates move in opposite directions. Lower interest rates are favorable for bonds for an investor. However, high interest rates increase the attractiveness of new bonds because they must offer high returns to attract investors.

CHAPTER 13

CHOOSE THE BEST INVESTMENT OPTION

Investors are increasingly forced to choose from a proliferation of investment options. They also have to deal with contradictory advice on how to achieve their financial goals and how to invest the savings they have accumulated during their lifetime.

If you consider that there are more than 7000 mutual funds available in the United States alone, and thousands of insurance products worldwide, making the choice that will satisfy them ever after is daunting, to say the least.

No wonder people so often ask the rather general question: Which investment is best? The first part of the answer is easy: No single investment is 'the best' under all circumstances for all investors. Personal circumstances, goals and different people's needs differ, as do the characteristics of different investments.

Secondly, one asset class's strength in certain circumstances could be another's weakness. It is therefore important to compare investments according to relevant criteria. The art is to find the appropriate investment for each objective and need.

The following are the most important criteria:

- The goal of the investment

- The risk the investor can handle

- Liquidity required

- Taxability of the investment

- The period until the financial goal is reached

- Last but not least, the cost of the investment.

THE GOAL

Goals determine the characteristics sought in an investment. You will be in a position to choose the most appropriate investment only when you have decided on your short-, medium- and long-term goals. The following generic goals are normally involved:

Emergency fund

Emergency fund money should be readily available when needed, and the value of the fund should be equal to about six months' income. Money market funds are excellent for this purpose. While these funds do not perform much higher than inflation, their benefit is that capital is saved and is easily accessible.

If you already have a ready emergency fund covering more than six months' income, you could consider a more aggressive mutual fund

Capital protection

If your primary aim is capital protection, you will have to be satisfied with a lower growth rate on the investment. Those above 50 are normally advised to be conservative in their investment approach.

While this may for the most part be sound advice, you should also keep an eye on the risk of inflation, so that the purchasing power of your money does not depreciate.

It is not the nominal value of the capital that should be protected, but the inflation-adjusted one. At an annual inflation rate of 6%, $1 million today will buy the same as $174 110 in 30 years' time. A 50 year-old with $1 million would therefore have to lower his living standard substantially if he only retains the $1 million until he was 80.

Conservative investments like those listed above should form the normal basis for providing an income. Because of inflation risk, investments should be structured so that they can at least keep up with inflation.

This means that at least a percentage of the investment source providing the income should be made up of other asset classes like property and equity mutual funds. The percentage would differ according to individual and economic circumstances.

Investors fortunate enough to have their basic budget provided for by a conservative fund could consider increasing their income with commercial property funds and tax-free income from dividends paid out by listed shares.

Capital growth

If an investor's primary goal is to achieve capital growth, the real rate of return should be higher than inflation. This implies greater risk to capital in the short term. Investors aiming at capital growth should not be apprehensive, as they will reap the rewards in the long term.

The history of equity prices over the past 100 years proves equity investments to be the best performer, followed by property. This does not mean you should buy either of these investments blindfolded. Wait until the quality shares in which you are interested are trading at inexpensive price levels.

RISK

The investment with a history of the highest growth is not necessarily the one to choose. The Standard Bank's Gold Fund increased by 178% during the period 13 August 2001 - 24 May 2002 (284 days). Judging only on the growth of the fund during this period, it performed exceptionally well.

But would it be the right investment for a retiree? During the 805 days following this, the same fund experienced a negative growth rate of 44%.

The problem with an investment that decreases by this percentage is that it will not reach its previous peak by increasing again by 44%. This is because the growth this time will take place from a lower base, so in fact the investment would have to increase by approximately 80%.

LIQUIDITY

Hard assets like Persian carpets, works of art and antique furniture may be good investments in the long term, but unfortunately they are not very liquid. The same is true of certain shares in smaller companies.

Money market funds, on the other hand, are very liquid, but the returns may not always be as good as those from other investments. The need to liquidize the investment quickly is therefore also a criterion to consider when evaluating investments.

TAXABILITY

The taxability of an investment has a considerable impact on its value to the investor. When comparing the returns on different investments, the return after tax has been deducted should be used. The investor should always ask what will be left in his pocket after tax deduction.

PERIOD

Conservative investments with no potential for high returns are suitable for shorter periods, while investment-objectives with longer time horizons aspire to achieving higher returns. Money market funds are suitable for periods of one or two years.

Income and conservative asset allocation funds for three or four years and flexible asset allocation funds, commercial property funds and value equity funds may be chosen for longer periods, dependent on the economic and interest cycle and the propensity of the investor to accept risk.

COSTS

The costs involved in an investment are normally things like administrative cost and commission. The percentage of the costs to the investment amount directly affects the value of the investment. Many of the currently available investment products are structured in such a way that investors can negotiate commission.

No investment strategy blueprint is going to be perfect for everyone's circumstances. Investment opportunities should therefore be examined critically before any decision is made. It should also be kept in mind that there are different companies managing specific funds under the investment categories referred to above.

Some are more effectively managed than others. Investors should therefore research investments as well as the managers thoroughly before investing. Otherwise, they could appoint professional asset managers to do so on their behalf. Time spent determining the type of investment you really need is time invested in your future financial well-being.

CONCLUSION

As a new investor, you need to learn to invest money before you start investing for retirement or any other financial goal. As a new investor you may not be able to find a financial planner you can work with or afford. Even if you found one, do you really want to start investing money with him or her without first getting your feet wet in the basics of personal investing.

Before you get into financial concepts like asset allocation and strategy, you should first learn the very basics: investment characteristics. How can you compare various alternatives to determine which best suit your needs, financial goals and comfort level?

In other words, you need to decide what you are really looking for. And you need a list of factors to consider before you start investing money. For example, do you have a long term goal like retirement, and are you willing to accept a moderate level of risk? If so, there are numerous investment alternatives to consider, and you can also get tax breaks.

On the other hand, if you have a shorter term financial goal and might need access to your money at a moment's notice, that's a totally different picture.

You need to match your financial wants and needs to the various alternatives that have characteristics best suited to your personal investing goals. There is no single best choice for every financial goal. It's a matter of give and take.

In this book, I have a list listed a lot of factors you must consider and a few other things you should consider before making a decision. This is basic investing 101. Whether you are a new investor or you've been at it for a while and have never really taken the time to learn to invest, you should learn the basics.

Don't feel bad if you are an uniformed new investor (or a want to-be). Do something and learn to invest starting with the basics.

Once you have a handle on a few basic financial concepts you can start investing with confidence. Once you learn to invest you can reach your financial goals. If you think I'm trying to build your confidence, you are right. Best of Luck.

www.ingramcontent.com/pod-product-compliance
Lightning Source LLC
Chambersburg PA
CBHW030518220526
45464CB00006B/2857